D1180504

CAUTIONARY VERSES
AND
RUTHLESS RHYMES

CAUTIONARY VERSES
AND
RUTHLESS RHYMES

Charlie Ottley

With illustrations by Oliver Preston

CONSTABLE · LONDON

Constable & Robinson Ltd
3 The Lanchesters
162 Fulham Palace Road
London W6 9ER
www.constablerobinson.com

First published in the UK by Constable,
an imprint of Constable & Robinson Ltd, 2006

A copy of the British Library Cataloguing in
Publication Data is available from the British Library.

ISBN-13: 978-1-84529-280-5
ISBN-10: 1-84529-280-4

Printed and bound in the EU

1 3 5 7 9 10 8 6 4 2

I want to dedicate this book...

To my parents who never stopped believing in me.

To my sister, without whom none of this would
have happened.

To Sarah, who should have been here.

To my friends, whose patience and encouragement has been
an inspiration and a guiding light –
in particular Bill, Nick, Shauna, James and
Row, Tim, Ali, Dom, Miles and Helen,
Toby, Damian and Geordie.

CONTENTS

CAUTIONARY VERSES

CONTEMPORARY MOMENTS

ACKNOWLEDGEMENTS

With thanks to Richard Ayers,
Portal Director at Tiscali

& Paul Sommers, Head of Factual
at Tiger Aspect Productions.

CAUTIONARY VERSES

14

THE TRAGIC TALE OF SALLY PLATT

WHO LIKED TO CHAT

POOR Sally was a lovely child,
Complexion fair and temper mild.
She was, it comes as no surprise,
The apple of her parents' eyes
Who gave her with a grateful sigh
Those things that only love can buy
Like Barbie and a matching Ken,
A hamster with revolving den,
A CD player made by Sony,
Two Furbies and My Little Pony.

In fact when there was cash to spare
Sweet Sally had the lion's share.

Their angel pops, their shining pearl
Became a most demanding girl
Who couldn't bear to be alone
So Santa brought a mobile phone.
Her mum and dad, on meagre means,
Were rapidly reduced to beans,
In part because they didn't know
About the new 'pay as you go'
But chose instead to foot the tab
For little lambykins to blab.

One day her dad received a bill
Which on digestion made him ill.
He double-checked the monstrous tally
And looked severely down at Sally.
Yet did his precious cherub balk?
No sir, she said, 'It's good to talk!'

It happened that, a few weeks later,
Young Miss Platt stormed out on mater.
Rudely slamming shut the door,
She walked down to the garage for
Some gum and, it can't be denied,
The better line she got outside.

Then calling up her sidekick, Pat,

The whining and ungrateful brat

Offloaded on her trusty mate

A bellyful of angst and hate

Directed at her mum, and said,

'I wish the silly cow was dead!'

On finishing her conversation

Sally reached the filling station.

Ignoring, though she should have known,

A sign that read 'Switch off your phone'.

She paid no notice – what a chump!

Just as she passed the petrol pump

Her mobile rang, produced a spark

Which very quickly found its mark.

Yes, with a deep and throaty cough

The phone was finally turned off,

As girl and forecourt, cars and all
Exploded in a blazing ball
Reducing half the street to rubble.
The fire brigade had major trouble.

As for Sally – well it's said

They never did retrieve her head!

No moral need be mentioned here,

The message of our tale is clear,

Except to add that at the wake,

While mum took round the tea and cake,

She stifled once upon a while

The faintest traces of a smile.

DANIEL SHRIVER, THE HOPELESS SKIVER

WHO MET A GHASTLY END PURSUANT
TO HIS LOVE OF PLAYING TRUANT

THIS is the tale of Daniel Shriver,

A burly, surly, little skiver

With almost no regard for rules,

Expelled from several public schools

At twenty thousand pounds a year

For getting drunk and smoking gear.

His dad by gradual degrees

Grew more resentful of the fees

As Daniel showed complete immunity

To privilege and opportunity,

Enjoying nothing more beyond

Those precious chances to abscond.

Alas one day it came to pass

He skipped a double physics class –

'How current is derived and stored' –

The sort of thing that left him bored.

'Who cares, it's electricity
Watt-ever!' he declared with glee.
Because of this Dan never heard
How electricity's transferred,
Six ways of generating power
And other facts that filled the hour.

But undeterred he chose to shirk it.

He missed how charge moves through a circuit,

How static is produced by nylon.

Instead he chose to climb a pylon,

Announcing, with his top lip curled,

'You learn more from the outside world!'

And yet as you may now discern

He didn't have much time to learn.

Sadly, fifty thousand volts

Gave him the most severe of jolts.

His skin turned black, his eyes went pop,

But still poor Daniel didn't drop.

He hung there sizzling like a roast

Until the hapless boy was toast.

MIRANDA

AND THE DANGERS OF LETTING YOUR CHILD
WATCH FILMS UNSUPERVISED

THEY SAY that movies can inspire

Behaviour sinister or dire,

As in the case of dear Miranda

Whose gentle innocence and candour

Were sullied by the motion picture.

Where viewing is devoid of stricture

One simple fact remains immutable

Kids will watch what's most unsuitable.

Miranda's foolish ma and pa

Permitted her Sky Cinema

And in her bedroom – most unwise –
Their doting girl would feast her eyes
On shocking images depicted
In films certificate, Restricted,
With content you'd describe as graphic
Erotic (hetero and sapphic)
Or bloody, gross and steeped in gore.
In no time poor Miranda saw
A spate of adult-rated horror:
Revenge of Sodom and Gomorrah
Ice Pick Tarts and *Psycho Nun.*
She thought them all tremendous fun,
For very little else compared
With feeling well and truly scared

Until it happened last Noel

She watched, *Infanti-claus From Hell!*

In which our Yuletide icon gains

A taste for young and healthy brains.

This gave her such a nasty fright

She couldn't sleep without the light.

Her choice of film as usual had

Escaped the notice of her dad

Who, sparing no expense to pander

To the whims of poor Miranda,

Had hired a shiny Santa suit

And crept upstairs with sacks of loot.

He edged towards his sleeping daughter

Armed with presents that he bought her

But tripped upon an empty cup

Which broke and quickly woke her up.

She surfaced from a fevered dream

With a loud and piercing scream

That almost stopped poor daddy's ticker.

Her eyes wide open in a flicker

Beheld the face of Santa Claus.

The frightened urchin didn't pause,

She grabbed the lamp beside the bed
And swung it at his bearded head.

There was a crash, there was a thud,

There was an awful lot of blood,

And by the time he hit the floor

Her wretched father was no more!

THE TALE OF LITTLE JAMES
WHO JUST ADORED COMPUTER GAMES

SINCE Jimmy was a baby boy
His mum and dad failed to employ
The necessary discipline.
Instead whenever he'd begin
To stamp his feet and wail and fret
They'd rush down to the shops and get
A fist of new computer games.
Whereupon their darling James
Would sit cross-legged and serene
Before the television screen.

He played them all, from outer space
To every kind of urban chase,
And savoured with a special relish
The ones most violent and hellish.
Indeed when in concern his dad
Would try to interrupt the lad
He'd mutter, underneath his breath,
'Shut up, papa, eat napalm death!'

As he grew older, things got worse,
He quite cleaned out his mother's purse
And raised such a tremendous stink
He drove his father back to drink.

The only time the little fool

Had some comeuppance was at school.

His interests did not make amends

For James's noted lack of friends.

In fact the other boys would taunt

This spotty youth, his pallor gaunt,

Framed by the most enormous specs

Due largely to the ill effects

Of staring at a screen all day

Instead of healthier forms of play.

And so it was as he matured

The misanthropic nerd endured

Such kickings, misery and hurt
It made him still more introvert.
While in his teens, his hormones raged
Yet new found lust was unassuaged.
For James was just so maladjusted
All the girls for whom he lusted
Hurried past him, quite disgusted.
In fact the only lass he trusted,
The one whose love he held aloft,
Went by the name of Lara Croft,
The only one who understood,
The only one he knew who would

Be there in just a single flick,

His virtually perfect chick.

These days the teenager has grown

But far from being all alone

I hear he frequently gets laid
And is, my sources tell me, paid
A figure that is quite obscene
By some computer magazine
For sitting smugly on his haunches
Playing all the latest launches
And writing dissolute reviews
Under the title *Gaming News.*

The moral of my tale is clear
And any parents please adhere:
If you spoil your child, be wise
Enough to let him specialize

For in this cut-throat day and age

At lease it guarantees a wage!

THE MALODOROUS TALE OF NATHAN STILL

AND HIS CONTRIBUTION TO WORLD PEACE

YOUNG Nathan Ebeneezer Still
Was gifted and could fart at will
Loud ones, odorous or quiet,
Quite irrespective of his diet.
This talent would elicit cheers
From jealous and admiring peers.
Adults winced and clutched their nose
As gleefully he'd strike a pose,

His elbows crooked like Rodin´s 'Thinker',

To drop a monumental stinker,

Inducing those nearby to fume

And rapidly vacate the room.

Nate's parents hired a host of quacks

To get his colon to relax

But no prescription could usurp

The very slightest bottom burp…

Meanwhile, and not yet connected,

The bullet-headed dunce elected

Leader of the GOP

Self-styled defender of the free

(that's free to have the extra fries

upgrade, consume and supersize,

burn petrol, buy a bigger truck,
spend every single borrowed buck
on therapists and holidays
and find more convoluted ways
to navel gaze and self-obsess,
to start each sentence with 'I guess',
to intervene in world affairs
but only when it bolsters shares
to countersue your wife and kids
and rig your own election bids)
That scourge of folks who deal in terror,
The guy that put the 'er...' in error,

Just survived, because he hid,

A botched assassination bid

And wanted, being paranoid,

To see the Middle East destroyed.

He hatched a plan called Project Valor

To 'blow those heathens back to Allah!'

Involving WMDs,

A move not guaranteed to please,

And one that would for certain bring

Retaliation from Beijing

And sternest disapproval from

Those not placated with a bomb,

The one exception being Britain

Who was beyond all logic, smitten.

Now as it happened just before

This goon could launch his holy war

The backward, thimble-minded klutz

Proposed new education cuts

To fund his weapons programme and

To give some friends a helping hand.

There was a suitable campaign

Along the lines of 'Brawn & Brain!'

With visits, trips and one concerning

Master Nathan's seat of learning.

They had a line up with the press,

A badly autocued address,

A meet and greet with senior staff,

Then kids could get an autograph.

Well Nate was early in the queue

He pushed and shoved and grunted through.

Confronted by the head of state

His insides started to gyrate

He accidentally let one slip,

There was the most colossal rip.

The sound of fabric singed and torn

Combined with something like a horn,

In short the sort of dreadful noise

That rarely hails from little boys.

The president was weak of heart

And when he heard this monster fart

Resounding like a pistol crack,

Mistook it for a fresh attack.

His stomach tightened and convulsed

His pulse rate well and truly pulsed,

He howled in pain and clutched his chest

Consumed by cardiac arrest.

He fell in spasms on the grass
And died, because of Nathan's arse.

So mums and dads, do not berate
Your children for an ugly trait,
For fate can often intervene,
Give noxious clouds a silver sheen,
As in the case of Nathan Still
Whose rare and most unusual skill,
Though not of course to be endorsed,
Preserved us all from holocaust

And, irrespective of your view,

The world's most lethal human who

Now buffs a small celestial harp

Thanks to a loud and timely pharp!

The Dangers of a Silly Name

Uranus Renaissance Parr
Was daughter to a movie star
And saddled with a nomenclature
Denotive of her social stature.
Her mum, a seventies screen diva,
Claimed to be a strong believer
In some new age cult called Flames,
Thus fond of more unusual names.

She thrust her baby from word go
Upon the pages of *Hello!*
For knowing what the scoop was worth
She let the press attend the birth.
It made a rather ugly spread
But earned her burned out mum some bread.

All through her early years at school
Uranus suffered ridicule.
Nicknames that were frankly heinous,
Like Space Freak, Alien and Anus.

She was in many different ways
Singled out for scorn or praise
And special treatment which, in truth,
Corrupts the innocence of youth.

Now I hear she's twenty-two
And not a bit like me or you.
The social highlights in her diary
Include long sojourns at The Priory.
Her nasal membrane's shot to hell,
She's almost lost her sense of smell
And, according to the *Sun*,
Last nostril count, she's down to one.

Tempting though it is to gloat,

Let's finish on a happy note.

You will, I'm sure, be most relieved

That when she recently conceived

A bouncing, bawling baby boy
She had the sense to call it Roy.

THE AWFUL FATE OF SANDRA BLACK
THE HOPELESS HYPOCHONDRIAC

THE British male too often whinges
When the slightest cough infringes
Upon his fragile habitat.
He starts believing, 'Well, that's that!'
He moans, he wails, curls up his toes,
Retires to bed to blow his nose
And watch the sport on daytime telly,
Feeding his distended belly
With Lucozade and crisps and snacks,
Insisting that he must relax.

And yet such stereotypes grow pale

Before the subject of this tale,

The much lamented Sandra Black,

A witless hypochondriac

Of quite the most persistent sort

Who almost permanently thought

She was about to meet her maker,

Compelling mother dear to take her

Down to the local surgery

Where, ignorant of perjury,

She'd manufacture a condition

To shock the resident physician.

This meant that as a general rule
Sandra spent whole weeks off school.
'I can't go in, I'm sick!' she blubbered,
Reaching for the bathroom cupboard
To pop another aspirin
And check the colour of her skin.
To help, she'd rub and squish her eyes,
Poke glands until they swelled in size
To guarantee her looks complied
With how she thought she felt inside.
While showing early signs of stealth,
She flicked through Blunt's *Domestic Health*

For symptoms of less usual types
To add more credence to her gripes.

At length the doctors all got wise
To Sandra's time-consuming lies.
They did their damndest to advise
A simple course of exercise
But Mrs Black refused to learn
And was too worried to discern,
Despite the fuss her child was making,
The chance her daughter could be faking.
She rushed to find the latest cures,
A favourite at the chemist stores,

She put her bank account in red
While Sandra lazed at home in bed
With magazines and Sky TV.

One week her usual GP
Was substituted by a locum
Who failed to see through Sandra's hokum
And, hearing her absurd complaints,
Including coughing blood and faints,
Decided in a trice that she
Should go at once to A&E.
'About time!' Sandra cried imperiously.
'Finally someone takes me seriously!'

Well much, much later on that day,

After a twelve-hour delay,

The self-indulgent little wally

Reclined triumphant on a trolley.

They wheeled her to a filthy ward

Where she was poked and pulled and pawed

And prodded in unpleasant places

But no one could find any traces

Of malaise, but thought it might

Be wise to keep her overnight.

It was, although the shortest stay,

Enough to catch MRSA.

Yet when she woke and cried in pain

Her feeble protests were in vain

And by the time the doctors checked

They were unable to affect

The end result, the cruellest fate,

A semi-vegetative state.

She doesn't blink or move her lips,

Hooked up to several different drips,

She spends her days awake, aware
But paralysed so cannot share
The fact that she is still alert.
And while of course it doesn't hurt,
She isn't what you'd label well,
Nor can the wretched urchin tell
Her nurses that she's feeling ill
Or reach for yet another pill
Or wince, or moan, or even cough.
Let's only hope they switch her off!

THE LUBRICATED CAREER OF BARCLAY DALE

AND HOW UNDERAGE DRINKING DOES NOT

ALWAYS LEAD TO RUIN

THIS is the most unlikely tale
Of Barclay Amyrillis Dale
Whose father held the latest views
On introducing kids to booze
And so would very often treat
His son to wine, both red with meat
And white, as fine as you could wish,
With poultry, pasta, pork or fish.

From Pinot Noir to Cabernet
He sampled every fine cuvée,
A kindness one might not deplore
Except the sorry lad was four!
And thus, as you may well divine,
A simple case of pearls and swine.
Although this was a shameful waste
Young Barclay soon acquired the taste

For everything from gin to beer.

His dad refused to interfere,

Not wishing to subvert or taint

His son's attempts to learn restraint.

By the time the lad was eight

He wasn't in a happy state.

At best his self-control was iffy.

At Sunday lunch he'd sit there squiffy,

Half cut and inclined to mumble

When not unconscious in the crumble.

And Mondays on the way to school

He'd clutch his head and moan and mewl,

Provoking mother to exclaim,

'You've only got yourself to blame!'

By twelve his teachers voiced concern

That Barclay didn't wish to learn,

While obviously his teenage years

Bore confirmation of their fears,

A period I won't describe

(He just continued to imbibe),

Becoming, well, a drunken lout.

In time his parents threw him out.

With no diplomas or degrees
And just one field of expertise
Poor Barclay didn't have much choice.
He picked the plum out of his voice
And chose the one place he could be,
That clinic called the BBC,
Where naturally the lad was groomed.
In comfort his decline resumed,
He's now an on-screen connoisseur
And can be seen to cause a stir
At viticultural events
With similar flamboyant gents.
Of course his thirst is still immense,
However there's the recompense:

When he commences to talk pap

Those present are obliged to clap!

The Tale of Keith

and why children should be discouraged

from being cruel to other beasts

Children really should refrain

From causing other creatures pain

For age will oft exaggerate

A defect or unpleasant trait,

Expanding what may lie beneath

As in the tragic case of Keith.

He loved all creatures great and small

In ways quite certain to appal

And cause one to avert one's eyes,

From pulling wings off dragonflies

To torching birds' nests, smashing eggs,

Divesting crane-flies of their legs,

Squashing toads completely flat

And rubbing mustard on the cat.

How different would his fate have been

Had mother thought to intervene

Or given him some proper toys.

Instead she said, 'Boys will be boys'

And left him to his own devices,

Heedless of potential crises.

Keith's habits worsened as he grew.

He fashioned blowguns from bamboo

And worried sheep with poisoned darts

And set a match to horses' farts

And learned a host of other tricks
With penknives, wire and sharpened sticks.
Yes as the little tyke got bigger
His viciousness increased in vigour
And by the time he finished school
Keith was interminably cruel.

He vowed to spend his gap year clubbing;
That is, administering a drubbing
To a cute and fluffy seal
Held irresistible appeal.

So forcing poor papa to pay,

He took a trip to Hudson Bay

To get up close with Genus Phoca

And turn those icecaps red and ochre.

In days of putting out the feelers

He hooked up with a gang of sealers.

For months Keith found unrivalled joy

In their despicable employ,

Participating in the culls

Clubbing cubs and smashing skulls,

And loving it, which wasn't nice.

And then one day out on the ice

A fog rolled in across the sea

Destroying visibility.

His colleagues cried, 'We have to go,'

But Master Keith refused to slow,

His face aglow with wicked zeal,

He shouted back, 'Just one last seal.'

Keith raised his heavy club once more

When from the mist there came a roar.

All anyone could do was stare

As an enormous polar bear

Lumbered from the gloom at Keith.

It put his head between its teeth.

The others screamed, some lost their lunch

On hearing the ensuing crunch

As mighty canines pierced his neck

And no one hung around to check

If Keith was dead, or simply maimed,

For which of course they can't be blamed.

His fate was well and truly sealed

And thus our moral is revealed:

If you let your child turn feral

Be sure you do so at their peril.

ANNE AND HER PERFECT MAN

WHEN Anne was young she'd often swoon
To Barbara Cartland, Mills & Boon
And treasured nothing else above
Those tales of deep, gut-wrenching love.
Her mum insisted from the start
That she ignore her fickle heart
And not let cupid be her master,
Maintaining, 'It will bring disaster.
For men are bad and men are evil,
Men bring trouble and upheaval.
So put them firmly in their place,
Essential for the human race

But otherwise of little use

Except to make the garden spruce

And bank accounts as lush and green

So someone else can cook and clean

While you can look pristine and be

The envy of society.'

Well Annie listened hard and tried

To keep her feelings locked inside.

She had a first love and a second

But every time that romance beckoned

She took such an objective stance

Her suitors didn't stand a chance,

As she resolved in every case

The noughts weren't in the proper place

And so would tactfully defer

Until one day Anne met a sir,

A man of circumstance exceeding

With apparent wealth and breeding,

Sir Peregrine Coles-Bosworth-Smee,

A bounder of the first degree,

Who swept her off her dainty feet

With whispered nothings, fair and sweet.

He swore to love her like no other

While Annie murmured, 'Thank you, mother!'

But ere the nuptial bells could ring

Coles-Bosworth-Smee had had a string

Of highly secretive affairs.

Each time he'd shower and pluck the hairs

From his Armani velvet jacket,

For Anne was worth a pretty packet,

Returning home with wine and flowers

For 'working' all those extra hours.

He seemed alarmingly sincere

And birds continued to appear

'Til halfway through their second year

When Anne discovered to her shock

She was perceived a laughing stock

By other ladies of society

Aware of Perry's impropriety.

That night he was as usual late,

But choosing to sit up and wait,

She vowed to make her spouse confess,

So went to fetch her wedding dress

Where it was rotting in the attic

To make things slightly more emphatic.

She put it on, plus the tiara,

Applied some lipstick and mascara

And draped herself on the chaise longue,

Appalled but trying to be strong.

In due course Peregrine crept in,

Attempting not to make a din,

But nothing could prevent the shriek

As spectre-like, she rose to speak.

'How could you? After what we've had?'

She told the unrepentant cad,

'And what we've done and what you've said,

And then to come back home to bed,

I really don't know how you could.

Was it worth it, were they good?

Just tell me honestly, please, Perry!'

To which he softly answered, 'Very!'

And so, it pains me to impart

The scoundrel broke her fragile heart.

Since then she's put our sex to use

In ways encroaching on abuse

And though she's rich, there's just one hitch,

Poor Anne's become an utter witch

Whose coldness is a form of blindness

Bereft of gentleness and kindness.

She's found herself a millionaire

For whom she doesn't really care.

According to their Swiss au pair,

Who very rarely says a word,

Her ladyship was overheard

Expounding to her only child

That men should always be reviled!

ISADORA

BEHOLD the soap-mad Isadora,

See the way her mates ignore her.

She doesn't notice their derision

Because to her they are less real

Than people on her television

For whom she cannot help but feel

Emotions plentiful and various.

While sharing their fictitious lives

Her own grows ever more vicarious.

EastEnders, Lost, Footballers' Wives,

A spate of rubbish every week

From *Emmerdale* and *One Tree Hill*

To *Hollyoaks* and *Dawson's Creek*

Or *Angel, Casualty, The Bill,*

So much distraction that I fear

Poor Isadora's barely here

(And lacking any firm conviction

May in very little time

Become herself a work of fiction,

Remembered only as a rhyme.)

YOUNG MONTY

YOUNG Montague was clearly gay.
His parents looked the other way,
Though sometimes mother acquiesces
And allows him to try on her dresses.
Imagine then the colonel's shock
When, coming downstairs in a frock,
The heir to his ancestral patch
Wore earrings that just didn't match!

113

GAV THE CHAV

NOTE well the tale of Gavin Salt

Whose motto, 'not my f*****g fault!!'

Did nothing to divert the blame.

With several ASBOS to his name,

His local council thought it right

To give the townsfolk a respite

By sending him on holiday

As an incentive not to stray.

He told the scallies in his gang

'It's shibby, geezas, total nang,

They sez I is a social failure,
An' so I'm checkin' out Australia!'

And so he did, but while abroad
He tumbled off a mountain board
And landing in a mossy heap
Disturbed a King Brown snake asleep.
He screamed and cursed, the air turned blue
With words and phrases no one knew.
They rushed him to intensive care
With very little time to spare

But when the team of doctors tried

To question him, the lad replied,

'Bin paggin with a Ricki Lake.'

By which of course he meant the snake.

'And how exactly do you feel?'

They asked the little imbecile.

'Completely ripped, I wanna spew.'

They didn't have a Scooby Doo

And so were forced to stand and stare

As Gavin's strange vocabulaire

Proved insufficient to explain

The cause and nature of his pain.

His failure to communicate

Meant very soon it was too late

And everyone could only watch

As an unpleasant purple blotch

Spread up his arm and reached his head,

Rendering young Gav 'well dead!'

A moral here could be evinced

Except this anecdote is rinsed.

OPHELIA

OPHELIA'S terrified of germs.

See the desperate way she squirms

When on a field trip somewhere scenic

She slips in something unhygenic!

FATHER JERRY FITZ

IT may be just misplaced conjecture
But Jerry's mother's need to lecture
And specialize in castigation
Paved the way for his vocation.
For such was Mrs Fitz' obsession
With eliciting confession
She bordered on the evangelical
And often got a tad hysterical.
Her eyes bulged as she frothed and raved
Whenever Jerry misbehaved,

It rubbed off on the wretched creature,

He went on to become a preacher

Of the televisual ilk

In fiery robes of burnished silk,

And though I'm sure he'll go to hell
Meanwhile he's doing rather well
By telling viewers on TV:
'If you love Jesus, you love me
And if you love me let's rejoice.
Imagine me in a Rolls-Royce.
So praise the Lord and Holy Ghost
And put your money in the post.
The Good Book says don't be a hoarder,
No notes, just cheques or postal order
To Jesus, care of Father Fitz
PO Box 15, St Kitts.'

125

THE CONTINUED FALL OF THE HOUSE OF USHER

An author by the name of Poe
Recounts a tale of utmost woe
Pertaining to the House of Usher.
Like some tragedy from Russia
It lacks the happy ever afters,
Just death, dark lakes, and blackened rafters.
The basis of this yarn's correct
But one thing Poe did not suspect
Was that the bloodline hadn't died

For cousins on the mother's side
Endured, and to their mortal shame
Purloined this most prestigious name,
Quite ignorant of any curse
Theirs is the subject of this verse.

The present day descendants had
An only son, a timid lad
Called Timothy, their pride and joy,
And took great pains to shield the boy
From those experiences inclined
To fuel an independent mind.

His mother laboured to instil

The subjugation of his will.

'For your own good!' she'd always bray,

'And don't you dare to disobey!'

He never did. One day mama

Was forced to buy another car

And, being more than slightly strapped,

She took the last one to be scrapped.

Arriving at the wrecker's yard,

She parked with total disregard,

As only certain people can,

And marching off to find 'the man',

She told young Timmy to sit tight,

A phrase that would be proven right.

Now picture, if you will, dear friends,

A giant magnet which descends

And swings the last surviving Usher

Up and over to the crusher.

And yet the lad did not protest,

Convinced that mother must know best,

A sentiment so deeply felt

He merely checked his safety belt.

The car was lowered into place,

Clamped tight in a hydraulic brace

Which with a hiss began to squeeze.

Timothy pulled up his knees.

It did no good, the shriek of metal

Deafened mummy's little petal,

While amidst this dreadful din
The doors and roof came folding in.
I like to think before the end
That Tim had time to comprehend
Just maybe mummy might have boobed
Before the hopeless child was cubed.

If any moral should prevail
From this unappetizing tale
It is that children for their sakes
Should realize parents make mistakes
(And sometimes it can be expedient
To be a little disobedient).

And parents, those that haven't wished

To see their little darlings squished,

Should note that to protect and bind

Can stunt a self-sufficient mind!

BEASTLY MOMENTS

THE FIDDLESTONE CAT

HE will sit in the park

From mid-morning till dark

And expound on the things to be done

As he lies in the shade

Of an evergreen glade

Or reclines on a bench in the sun.

As he skims through the papers

And reads of the capers

Of the great and the good he'll agree

That he could do that

Says the Fiddlestone Cat,

'Yes I could do that!' says he.

Oh, he'll bask on the sidelines

And offers his guidelines

On every profession around

But you won't find him queuing

When something needs doing

He's nowhere at all to be found.

But when they start working

He'll saunter up smirking,

Declare with a deep sense of glee

That '*You've missed a bit there!*'

Or '*It doesn't look square!*'

Or '*You should have first run it past me!*'

With a sensuous purr

He will groom his sleek fur

Murmur, '*Such a great shame I'm not free,*

'*Cause I could do that!*'

Says the Fiddlestone Cat.

'*Yes, I could do that!*' says he.

Now his whiskers are brittle

His chin caked with spittle

He's lost several claws in the bark,

But he sits patiently

'Neath his favourite tree

And is still often heard to remark

As they talk of the tropics

Or famous biopics

Or some well deserved OBE,

'*I could have done that!*'

Adds the Fiddlestone Cat.

'*Yes, I could have done that!*' says he.

144

FOWL PLAY

(IT'S THE WAY YOU TELL 'EM)

LIBRARIES are always seen

As peaceful places, quiet, serene

Where figures whisper in unknown

To read or take a book on loan.

Yet once this sombre hall of learning

Became a place of gasps and gurning

As everyone had cause to pause

And turn towards the double doors.

Some laughed, while others, horror stricken,

Watched a large rust-coloured chicken

Enter and survey the room,

Then with a beady eye resume

Its journey, stately and burlesque,

Towards the information desk.

Well this particular librarian,

Who was an ardent vegetarian,

And religious studies teacher,

Respected every living creature,

But even she was lost for words

When this quite moderate of birds

Surveyed her with a steely look

And staring up, said quietly, 'Book!'

Now library rules are most specific,

Comprehensive and prolific

But there's nothing in the least

Regarding loans to bird or beast.

Still putting on her horn-rimmed specs,

She picks the ledger up and checks.

Confirming there's no written rule

She grabs the nearest opuscule,

Selected works by Molière,

And with a rather puzzled air

Hands it to our feathered freak

Who takes the volume in its beak

And leaves with a contented cluck

While browsers murmur, 'What the …?'

Next day this peculiar hen

Returns said volume back again,

Dropping it upon the floor

Then staring fiercely up once more

The plucky fowl exclaims, 'Book, book!'

Well our librarian forsook

Her usual calm unrattled guise.

She blinks, she stares, she rubs her eyes

And mutters in a voice unsteady,

'You mean you've read that one already?'

With an extremely puzzled frown

She grabs two books and hands them down.

With one tucked underneath each wing
It waddles out, unfaltering.
Again, next day, the chicken's back,
This time armed with canvas sack.
Returning former tomes, our chook
Predictably cries, 'Book, book, book!'

Astonished, the librarian delves

The sturdiest of library shelves

For volumes of a certain weight

In one last effort to frustrate

And presently returning brings

War and Peace, *Lord of the Rings*

Plus Shakespeare, *His Completed Work*

And hands them over with a smirk.

The chicken struggles bravely out,

It lumbers like a man with gout,

But carries its ungainly load

Through double doors and down the road.

Now curiosity, though bad for cats

Is slow to stir in bureaucrats

Yet finally our civil servant,

Although slow and unobservant,

Concluded with a tired sigh,

'It's time I found out where and why!'

She left her post to play the sleuth
And slipped unnoticed from her booth.
She tracked the chicken down the street
At distance suitably discreet
Until it reached the village pond.
It dropped the books, looked out beyond
To where a water lily flowered
And half-submerged a rotted log
Upon which sat and spat and glowered
A large and most repugnant frog.

Once more the chicken cleared its throat
And uttered in a piercing note

So forcibly its feathers shook

The latest mantra, 'Book, book, book.'

The frog, its chest puffed out in pride,

No sooner than the chicken said it,

With an angry croak replied,

'Read it, read it, read it!'

SAMANTHA

SAMANTHA had reached that intolerable age
Where she wanted a zoo-full of pets,
But she couldn't be bothered to clean out
their cage
So they all took a trip to the vet's.

PIONEERING MOMENTS

The Tale of Running Bear

Big chief Running Bear
Was getting desperate for an heir,
His clan was blessed with many squaws,
All of whom had dropped their drawers
And laboured hard with little thanks
While he continued to fire blanks.
Now his was not a happy state
For every brave must procreate.
Apache, Navajo or Sioux
Whatever tribe, this rule holds true.
When your survival is relying
On going forth and multiplying

To lack a son is just not done,

Especially as number one

Head honcho and the local chief

Your reign is likely to be brief

Devoid of any pension schemes

And liable to end in screams.

Already Running Bear was snubbed

And certain dissidents had dubbed

Him cruelly Big Chief Empty Quiver,

Predicting he would not deliver.

Finally in fear he went

And visited his shaman's tent

To ask advice and to implore

His loyal wise man for a cure.

Upon unburdening his soul

The shaman handed him a bowl

Of rather bitter cactus juice

Which made him sick and turned him puce

And filled him with the urge to dance

Before collapsing in a trance.

Whereafter the great god Peyote

Came to him as a coyote

And in an infant's voice decreed

That he revitalize his seed

And to ensure a healthy child

Invoke the spirits of the wild,

Which meant, of course, a sacred quest
To find new furs to line his nest,
The pelts of strange and mighty beasts
On which to share his carnal feasts.
Three animals he must procure,
Each powerful in tooth and claw.
The first two, easy to obtain,
The buffalo that roams the plain,
A scaly monster large and vile
Known mostly as a crocodile,
The third one caused a lot of fuss.
'What is a hippopotamus?'
He asked his transcendental guide.
'That's your concern,' the god replied.

Upon which Running Bear awoke

And raised his head as twilight broke

And rosy-fingered Dawn came round

But kisses fell on barren ground.

'Let go, Dawn,' he chastised his squaw.

'Not now, we've been through this before!

It doesn't work! I have to go.

Bring me my buckskin and my bow,

A mighty journey lies ahead

With many weary miles to tread.

Mine is a dark and risky course.'

This said he leapt upon his horse,

Dug in his heels and shouting, 'Hup',

He turned and told her, 'Don't wait up!'

Now Running Bear had no idea
In which direction he should steer
And very rapidly forthwith
Traversed into the land of myth.
The buffalo he found with ease
And skinned it up against two trees,
Then heading south, the legend speaks
Of how he rode for many weeks
'Till night and day began to swelter
And he approached a river delta
Not very far from the equator
Where chancing on an alligator
He took the general view that, while
It wasn't quite a crocodile,

Despite his otherworld advice,

In principle it would suffice.

The alligator, no surprise,

Was less inclined to compromise.

It struggled fiercely not to be

Matrimonial upholstery

And dragged him, flailing, underwater

But in the fury of the slaughter

Released him for a better grip,

Enabling Running Bear to slip

His hunting knife out of his belt

And thus the killing blow was dealt,

A corker, right between the eyes

And, judging by its ample size,

He'd quite enough to make a mat,

An overnight bag and a hat

Or handbag for his favourite squaw.

But now remained the toughest chore.

While its habitat's uliginous

The hippo's not indigenous

And though he oftentimes conferred

No one that he met had heard

Of genus Hippopotami

Besides one rather ancient guy

Of central African descent

Who told him gravely to relent.

But Running Bear took little heed

And, selling his beloved steed,

He built himself a fine canoe

And set off cross the ocean blue.

We can't be certain what took place,

Our hero vanished without trace

For six long months, and then one day

He staggered back on feet of clay,

Dragging a reluctant ass

Upon whose back was piled a mass

Of skins and tacky souvenirs.

The tribe assembled, screaming cheers,

But praises fell on deafened ears.

Their chief, ignoring the applause,

Turned to his three expectant squaws

And yawning said, 'I'm feeling sleepy.

Wives, please join me in my tepee.'

Several days and nights converged
Before a happy chief emerged,
Convinced that he had been redeemed.
And cured he was, or so it seemed,
For nine months on they'd all conceived
And everyone was most relieved.
The wife who slept on alligator
Sired a son, delighting pater.
The lass who laid on buffalo
Begat a girl as pale as snow.
Whereas the wife on hippo skins
Produced both in the form of twins.
Which goes to show, at some travail,
The central message of our tale:

That the squaw on the hippopotamus coincides

To the sum of the squaws on the other two hides.

Aussie Joke

This is one of those intriguing tales
Of three jackeroos from New South Wales
Who, getting paid each Friday night,
Would drive to Sydney for a fight
And, as was common in New South Wales,
More than a few revolting ales.
On this particular occasion
They spied an oddly dressed Caucasian
Slouched by the bar, a trifle merry,
On his seventh glass of sherry

So Terry, Bill and his mate Paul,

Those were their names as I recall,

Made their minds up to let rip

And give this guy a bit of jip.

So Paul walks up with a menacing gait

And says, 'G'day, how are you, mate?

Me and me pals, we was wondering why

You're dressed like that, it's offending the eye.'

But much to his shock and no little surprise

In a pommie accent the stranger replies,

'Indeed? Well you see, I'm a newcomer here

But do let me buy you the next round of beer.'

This thawed Paul's heart in one fell sweep

More surely than the softest sheep

And he exclaimed, ' I'll be a dingo,

You may talk odd, but that's my lingo.

So what's your line?' he asked in earnest.

'Well I'm just a taxidermist.

I stuff animals, it's true!

Last week I stuffed a kangaroo,

Three sheep, a wombat and what's more
A woman and her labrador.
So after that I thought it best
To take some time out for a rest.'
With admiration in his eyes,
Paul answered, 'I apologize'
And quietly rejoined his crew
Who muttered, 'What's got into you?
What the hell was that about?
I thought you said you'd sort him out!'
'Shut up,' cried Paul, 'The bloke's all right.
There's more deserving folks to fight.'

'Well,' said Bill, 'It's not like you.

Who was that guy, what does he do?'

'I think he's just a taxi driver.

I couldn't get his accent neither.

It was difficult with all that noise,

But apart from that he's one of the boys!'

TEXAS PETE

TEXAS Pete was one tough guy
Conceived beneath the desert sky.
His hands were huge, his knuckles hairy
From cowboy work out on the prairie.
His boots were worn, they gave him bunions
And corns adorned his feet like onions,
The soles so hardened underneath
A rattlesnake would break its teeth.
Yes, Pete was tough, perhaps uncouth,
But never failed to tell the truth,

Believing to escape the Devil

'A person must be on the level.'

Aside from sticking to his word

Pete's obligation was the herd.

Each day a new and different battle

To tend a thousand head of cattle,

To keep them fit and fat and perky.

At eventide he'd chew beef jerky

And poke the fire or watch the moon

And strum an idle little tune

Upon his battered ukulele,

Wondering and dreaming daily

Of the time he'd flog his stock

And hear the hammer on the block,

And feel the crisp of folded tender

For nights far from his hacienda.

You might perhaps be pleased to hear

That every single cow and steer

Was sold and fetched a tidy price

Which was, for Pete's sake, rather nice.

He'd cleared his debts and made a mint.

And now he hankered for the glint

Of liquid gold, the faithful grain

To dull the aches and numb the pain,

A good shag and a clean spittoon,

So made his way to the saloon.

A desperate man in desperate need,

He tied his true but stumpy steed

Securely to the hitching stick

And walked inside. The air was thick

With smoke and sweat and rancid liquor.

Silence thundered. In a flicker

Every punter, man and whore

Looked up as Pete came through the door.

The local gossips held their braying,

The poker players stopped their playing,

The pianist ceased his merry tinkling,

For everybody had an inkling

This guy was trouble, so to speak,

And not the sort you'd seek to pique.

The landlord struggled to his feet

And stared in fear at Texas Pete

Who hitched his gunbelt up a notch,

Took off his hat and whispered, 'Scotch.'

Well in a flash he downed the first

And, having got a mighty thirst,

Pete made the second one a double,

Then to avoid potential trouble

He downed a third and turned to go

And, straightening his hat real slow,

He walked into the afternoon

As talk resumed in the saloon.

Back on the street, Pete looked around.

He saw the post, the empty ground,

The rope still tied, except some fool

Had dispossessed him of his mule.

He turned back to the swinging door

And kicked it open with a roar.

The local gossips held their braying,
The poker players stopped their playing,
The pianist ceased his merry tinkling,
For all had more than just an inkling
The price of life, as weighed and reckoned,
Was getting cheaper by the second.

The landlord struggled to his feet.
He stared in fear at Texas Pete
Who said, 'Now, barman, listen here.
This time I think I'll have a beer
And if my mule ain't back and tied
By the time I step outside

It won't be nice, it won't be pretty,

Same as happened in Dodge City!'

Pete drank his ale, and left the place,

An icy scowl upon his face,

But when he got outside he saw

His mule tied to the post once more.

He mounted up for heading off.

Behind him came a quiet cough.

An old man in a wicker chair

Who'd overheard the whole affair

Said, 'Sorry, but before you go

There's just one thing I got to know.

You left them standing, more's the pity,

But pray, what happened in Dodge City?'

Well Pete leant over looking shy

And softly muttered his reply.

Now bear in mind he never lied

And more than that took certain pride

In having little time for talk.

He whispered back, 'I had to walk!'

CONTEMPORARY MOMENTS

THE COUNTRY GENT

THERE once was a country gentleman
In a well-to-do county down south.
Many people still tell stories
Of his raising money for the Tories.
At every house he'd have a glass.
He thought it most unkind to pass.
So many evenings would be spent
Drinking whisky for a government
With a 'Really, do I dare it'
And a 'Well, if you can spare it',

With a 'Since the bottle's open'

And a 'Pour me just a token'

'Til the cows came a rolling home.

There is no moral to my story,

Except that if you must vote Tory

Be careful not to make it known

Or you'll be drunk from house and home

With a 'Really, do I dare it'

And a 'Well, if you can spare it',

With a 'Since the bottle's open'

And a 'Pour me just a token',
With a 'Maybe just a fast one'
And 'This has to be the last one'
'Til the cows have come and gone.

George and His Pony Tony

The difficulty was with George
He had a tendency to gorge
And being not entirely bright
Could scarce control his appetite
Which mother would attempt to sate
By piling more upon his plate
Until the greedy boy turned puce
And blew up like a foie gras goose.
Now tubby children look obscene
And George was very far from lean.

His piggy eyes, his chubby arms
Further compromised his charms,
As did his thighs, which chafed and grated
When the boy perambulated.
Well daddy thought the best recourse
Would be to buy his son a horse

So he could go out for a ride
Instead of loitering inside
And be a man just like his pa
Or cowboys from the cinema.

So George was saddled with a pony
Which he chose to christen Tony.
Now George, like pappy, was no stranger
To 'history's heroes', the Lone Ranger,
Shane, Butch Cassidy or Zorro,
Names he'd regularly borrow
And chaps he'd try to imitate
When he rode out on dad's estate

To earn himself a brief reprieve

And play those games of make believe

Like 'Cowboys and non-Christian folks'

But each time it took more to coax

Poor Tony from his cosy stable,

As George's steed grew barely able

To bear his master's heavy weight.

For exercise just meant George ate

Lots more. To supplement his diet

He started bingeing on the quiet

On lard and crisps and Reece's Pieces,

Until his folds developed creases,

Ballooning in so many places

He found it hard to tie his laces.

One lunchtime, after six éclairs,

George paddled up the mounting stairs

And dropped onto the pony's back.

There was a loud and painful crack

As Tony with a final bray
Collapsed recumbent in the hay.

But Sampson-like he also threw

His nemesis, his Waterloo,

Across the barn, there came a scream

As George connected with a beam,

Then silence, thus our story ends,

As do two not-so-special friends.

IF...

IF you can keep your head when all about you

Are losing theirs and blaming it on you.

If you can trust yourself, when all men doubt you,

But make allowance for their doubting too.

If you can lie and not be tired of lying,

Or being lied about, and deal more lies,

Or being hated, don't give way to crying

And yet don't look too good, nor talk too wise,

If you can haunt the shadows of your masters
And with your silver tongue make fiction fact,
If you can meet with manifold disasters
And still resign instead of being sacked,
If you can bear to hear the lies you've spoken
Twisted by hacks to make a cunning trap
Or watch the things you gave your life to broken
And stoop to spouting more unbridled crap,

If you can make a heap of all your winnings
And risk the lot upon a dodgy loan
And be found out, return to your beginnings,
Yet never let your schemes be overthrown,

If you can force your heart, and nerve and cunning
To serve your turn long after you are gone,
And so hold on and still be in the running
Until the angry pundits cry, 'Hold on!'

If you can talk with Kings, reward their virtue
With passports, licences and laws
And, even when the consequences hurt you,
Wed private interest with the common cause,
If you can fill a telephonic minute
With sixty seconds-worth of flannel spun,
Yours is the EU, and everything that's in it,
And what is more you'll be a Mandelson.

MAD BRITAIN

(SOME RANDOM EXTRACTS FROM THE NEWS)

HAS local government gone bonkers,

Our children are at risk from conkers.

They make paths slippery to tread,

They fall and hit you on the head

So much that Norwich Council chose

To chop down several leafy rows

Of chestnut trees. Bravo, great stuff!

But, tell me, will that be enough?

My peace of mind won't be complete

'Till kids are taken off the street

And wrapped in cotton wool instead

And hidden underneath the bed.

IT COSTS three hundred thousand pounds

For Andrew Windsor's many rounds.

But what precisely does he do?

We don't appear to have a clue.

I'm sure he must have got a task.

And yet the only thing they ask

This dedicated island hopper

As he emerges from the chopper

Or clambers from his shiny Rolls,

'Will that be nine or eighteen holes?'

A NEW judicial ruling means

It could be fine to beat up greens,

To slash the leaf and grind the stem

And vandalize all things GM,

To pillage rape and savage maize

And have your nasty little ways

With veg that scientists have tampered

Carte blanche and legally unhampered,

Yes, spill the sap and let it trickle,

Wield your scythe and raise your sickle,

Open the sluices of vegetable juices,

Put to the torch these genetic abuses

And let those farms find better uses

For their land 'cause filling fields

With crops that promise mutant yields

Could lead to unimagined harm

Down on the old McFrankenfarm.

BEWARE the internet my child

Unless you wish to get beguiled

By crusty perverts who pretend

To be your very bestest friend

And once they've swept you off your feet

Suggest it would be fun to meet,

From whence there is no turning back.

He's fat, he's bald, he wears a Mac.

But maybe you should take some blame

To join some chat room with a name

Like Younger Girls for Older Guys

Cannot be deemed entirely wise.

DISRAELI, Winston, William Pitt
Had style and eloquence and wit.
The oratory of bygone days
Has been replaced with bland clichés,
Sentimental and contrite,
Reduced in essence to a byte
To clinch the deal and steal the show
With microphones that thrust and go,
The message stripped to barest bones,
A path of well-placed stepping stones,
Much safer than impassioned rant
To cross those streams of verbal cant
Untested, challenged and untried!
Because you see they're terrified

Of getting slated, sacked or sued,
Appearing unconcerned or rude
While speech is often misconstrued.
A sound-byte on the other hand
Can be meticulously planned
Like junk food – easy to digest
And as the papers will attest
Makes light the work of troubled sub,
Just quote, and head off down the pub!

IT'S NICE to know the NHS
Despite an ever-present mess,
The lack of staff, its dearth of space,
Is kind enough to find a place
And spend a portion of its dregs
On breaking (twice) a pair of legs
To help a little girl address
Her dream to be an airhostess.
I wonder if they'd be as nice
And break my skull and use a vice
To stretch my head, so I could be
A *Star Trek* extra on TV?

The Sun: a practical guide

The yellow dwarf above us runs
Upon six hundred million tons
Of hydrogen for every second,
So astronomers have reckoned.

The sun is not a solid mass
But one large ball of burning gas
With an incandescent girth
109 times our earth.

It takes eight minutes for the light

To cross the vast galactic night

Before it finally arrives

And feeds our frail organic lives.

With its warmth the sunshine brings

The energy for living things,

So does it seem remotely odd

Some cultures treat it as a god?

This object of barbaric prayers

Possesses three external layers

Or parts that we can see from here,
The first is called the photosphere.

According to the science manuals
The photosphere contains huge granules,
Bubbles that expand and flow
Bring up the heat and make it glow.

Being young the sun gets lots
Of dark and pretty heinous spots
Caused by strong magnetic fields.
Deflecting heat they act as shields.

Being cooler these appear
Much darker than the photosphere
And as they grow and group together
Sunspots can affect the weather.

Next there is the chromosphere
Which in eclipses can appear
A ring of vaguely pinkish light,
Much wider still but not as bright.

Beyond this the corona spreads
A pearly white above our heads.

Though dimmer it's the hottest place
Extending light years into space.

4.6 billion years of age
The sun is in its youthful stage.
Five billion more and the supply
Of hydrogen starts running dry.

To keep alight it switches fuel
To helium, a most uncool
And lively substance, which will trigger
The ageing sun to get much bigger.

As it expands, our planet fries,

The seven seas will vaporize

And be replaced with molten rock.

But no real need to watch the clock,

There's still a bit of time to spare.

But bear in mind that gentle glare

That warmed the rich primeval mud

Will one day roast us like a spud!

On Steven (Livingstone) Seagal

being named a reincarnated

Buddhist lama

I USED to be a Buddhist 'cause I thought it
would be great

To practise love and peace and stuff, and
learn to meditate.

I saved the spiders in the bath, I looked
each time I trod

For fear of stepping on an unsuspecting
arthropod.

I strove to find enlightenment and walk
the Middle Way

Until I bought a tabloid one portentous
winter's day

And there it was in writing, iridescent with
bad karma,

'Steven Seagal has been named a risen
Buddhist lama.'

'Surely not!' I muttered, but alas it was,
dear readers,

A serious decision by Tibetan Buddhist leaders.

I stormed, I raged, I cried aloud, ' I can't believe
they could ha'!'

The closest he has come to peace is…

'Buddha Buddha Buddha!'

THERE is no paper in the loo.

I knew I should have had a look

But now alas I'm halfway through

And will be forced to use this book.